Goalball

⑤

Contents

Written by Samantha Montgomerie

Collins

History of goalball

Goalball was invented in 1946 by Hanz Lorenzen and his friend Sepp.

Many **veterans** had lost their sight during the recent worldwide **conflict**, which ended in 1945. Hanz and Sepp wanted to help the veterans so they invented a sport for **sight-impaired** people.

What is goalball?

All players wear goggles so no one player can see better than any others.

Quiet please

Shhh! People are silent when watching a match so players can listen for the bell inside the ball.

Players must reach for the ball with their hands.

5

The aim of goalball is to earn the most points by throwing the ball into the other team's goal.

There are three players from each team on the pitch at one time.

Fact
Scoring: 1 goal = 1 point

Goalball pitch

Each side of the pitch is divided into three zones.

goal

team zone

landing zone

free zone

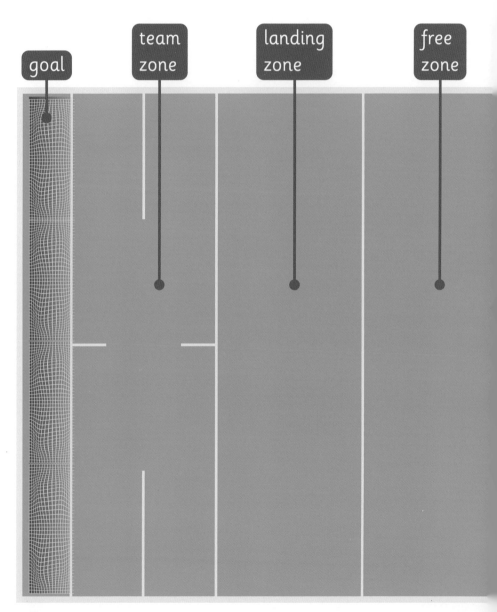

The floor has raised lines so players can feel where they are on the pitch. Goals at each end span the width of the pitch.

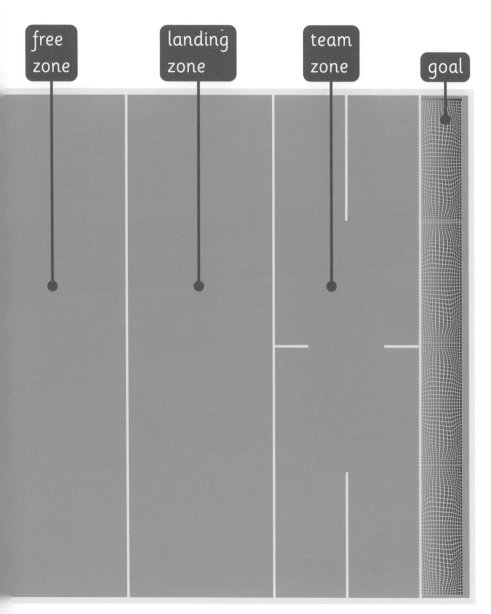

free zone

landing zone

team zone

goal

Playing a match

Defence players (the ones defending the goal) cannot **venture** down the pitch. They stay in the team zone.

The offence players (the ones trying to get a goal) must shoot from the landing zone.

The players spread out to avoid bumping into each other. When they hear the ball coming, they all stretch out wide across the floor.

Defending players want to capture the ball and
block the goal.

Players stretch out to block. They make their body as long as they can.

Playing safely

Players must block the hard ball if it gets near their goal, so they need to wear safety equipment.

padded trousers

elbow pads

Players spread their fingers wide to clutch the ball, then swing to throw!

When awaiting a shot, players must keep contact with the floor.

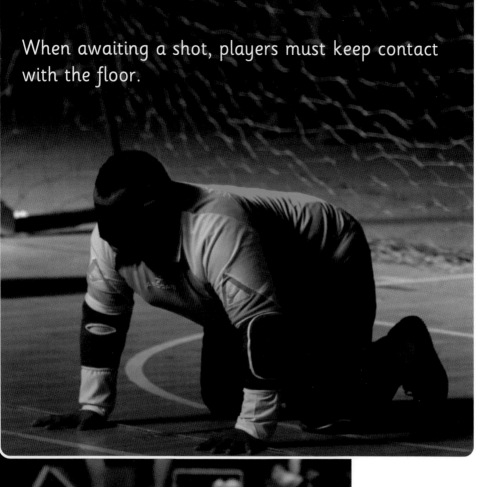

The teams switch ends at half-time.

If a team leads by ten points, the match finishes early and they win.

Rules

- A coin toss decides who starts with the ball.
- After a goal or a block, teams swap from defence to offence.

- No kicking!
- Underarm throwing and rolling only.
- There are only ten seconds to take a shot.

Glossary

conflict fighting, battles

sight-impaired refers to people who can't see
    well or are blind

venture to go bravely

veterans ex-fighters/ex-members of an army

Index

Goalball for everyone

Goalball is a lot of fun! By wearing a blindfold or goggles, lots of people can play this fast-paced and skilled game.

Everyone can share in the fun.

World's best goalball teams

These are the countries that have won
most gold, silver and bronze medals
at the Goalball World Games.

Number	Country	Gold	Silver	Bronze	Total
1	United States	4	2	2	8
2	Finland	2	0	1	3
3	Denmark	1	2	0	3

Spotlight on ... Jenny Blow

Jenny Blow is a top Goalball player. She has played in three Goalball World Games.

She won a scholarship to play while at university.

Jenny plays for the New South Wales Goalball team and has helped them win many medals.

Goalball

throwing

awaiting

blocking

stretching

scoring

🐾 Review: After reading 🐾

Use your assessment from hearing the children read to choose any GPCs, words or tricky words that need additional practice.

Read 1: Decoding

- Ask the children to read these words. Tell them to look out for the different ways in which the /ch/ and /air/ sounds are written.
  share   wearing   where   venture   switch   which
- Challenge the children to take turns to read a page as fluently as possible. Say: Can you blend in your head as you read aloud?

Read 2: Prosody

- Model reading pages 10 and 11 to the children as if you are presenting a video explaining the sport.
- Discuss how the phrases in the brackets are explanations, and are better read in a different tone to keep the rest of the sentence clear.
- Ask the children to take turns reading the sentences and discuss the effects of their use of pauses, tone, emphasis and pace.

Read 3: Comprehension

- Discuss children's favourite ball games and why they prefer them.
- Compare goalball to any other ball games the children are familiar with. Ask: In what main ways is it different to games like football? (e.g. *the players wear goggles so none of the players can see; the players rely on sound; spectators have to be silent*)
- Turn to page 17 and point to the word **contact**. Ask: What does it mean in the context of the sentence? (e.g. *keep touching*)
- Turn to pages 10 and 11. Compare **offence** and **defence**. Ask:
  o Where might you be when you throw? Where do we look to find out? (e.g. look for rules, headings, at photos – page 10: *defence players **stay in the team zone***)
  o Why is it important for defenders to wear pads? (e.g. *page 14: the ball is hard and they have to block it*)
  o What type of throwing is allowed? Where do we look to find out? (*look for the heading **Rules**; underarm throwing and rolling*)
- Turn to pages 30 and 31 and ask the children to talk about the different techniques needed to play goalball. What rules can they remember?
- Bonus content: Ask the children to reread pages 28 and 29. Ask: Can you find three reasons why Jenny Blow has been chosen for the "Spotlight". (e.g. *she is a top player; played three World Games; won a scholarship; helped a team win lots of medals*)